Starter Guide to Creating
ART QUILTS

Dr. Susan Kruszynski

Starter Guide to Creating Art Quilts

Landauer Publishing, www.landauerpub.com, is an imprint of
Fox Chapel Publishing Company, Inc.

Project Team
Editor: Sherry Vitolo
Copy Editor: Colleen Dorsey
Designer: Mary Ann Kahn

ISBN 978-1-947163-84-3

We are always looking for talented authors. To submit an idea, please send a brief inquiry to
acquisitions@foxchapelpublishing.com.

Note to Professional Copy Services:
The publisher grants you permission to make up to six copies of any quilt patterns in this
book for any customer who purchased this book and states the copies are for personal use.

Printed in Canada

This book has been published with the intent to provide accurate and authoritative information in
regard to the subject matter within. While every precaution has been taken in the preparation of
this book, the author and publisher expressly disclaim any responsibility for any errors, omissions,
or adverse effects arising from the use or application of the information contained herein.

Contents

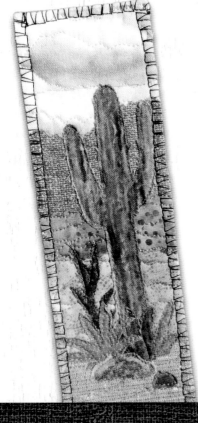

Introduction

Thank you for choosing to read *Starter Guide to Creating Art Quilts* and for inviting me to teach you the skills of art quilting through creating these projects. My goal is to add value to your life with what I share. *Starter Guide to Creating Art Quilts* will enhance your knowledge by answering the question, "What is an art quilt?" and will increase your skills by giving you easy steps to get you started in this beautiful quilting style.

Art quilting is a relatively new form of quilting, and the terms used to describe art quilting can be a bit confusing. When people ask me what I do, I jump into teacher mode to start defining my artform. The long answer is, "I am a collage landscape art quilter in the categories of fiber arts or textile arts." Come again? My short answer is, "I'm an art quilter."

{ "I'm an art quilter." }

DEFINITIONS

Fiber Arts/Textile Arts—Fiber arts and textile arts are both basically fabric artwork; the terms are used interchangeably.

Art Quilter—A quilter using both modern and traditional quilting techniques to create fabric artwork based on ideas and images rather than the repeated pattern of blocks found in traditional quilting.

Landscape Art or Landscape Art Quilting—Landscape art is a representation of natural scenery in art. The art may include mountains, water, fields, forests, flora, or fauna, and it may or may not include man-made structures or people.

Collage—Collages can be created from a wide range of materials, the most well-known being paper. For collages in art quilting, we use fabrics with or without fusibles applied to the backs of the fabrics. The word "appliqué" is very similar to the word "collage." Appliqué also means to decorate with pieces of fabric to form pictures or patterns. However, in the quilting world, appliqué often refers to applying pieces of fabric with rolled edges.

The term collage is both a work of art (noun) and a technique (verb) that you actively do; I collage (verb) to make an art collage (noun).

With this in mind, collage art quilting uses small pieces of fabric (raw edge and sometimes folded) grouped together to form a quilt top. It is a form of fiber art that looks like painting with fabric because the layering process and the final result are similar. For the purposes of this book, think of collage art quilting as painting with raw-edged fabric.

MY STYLE OF ART QUILTING

What is my style of fiber art or art quilting? My methods for creating a collage art quilt involve:

- Painting with fabric; each art quilt resembles a painting and is a totally unique work of art
- Pictorial quilting
- Sizes that range from very small to very large
- Three layers: (1) a cotton backing, (2) a piece of quilt batting or fusible fleece in the middle, and (3) a decorative top layer
- Collaging with fusibles atop the background layer—applying small fabric pieces backed with adhesives
- Raw edges on each piece of fabric (not rolled under). Often, my collages have raw-edged pieces, such as trees, leaves, plants, flowers, and other shapes

- Mostly cotton fabrics; manufactured and some hand-dyed, traditional quilting prints and "landscape" prints
- Using a basic home sewing machine for fussy machine stitching (not free motion, though it can be) with thread colors that accent the beauty of the fabric pieces and colors
- Different amounts of top stitching/thread painting to enhance art quilts
- Adding fabric paints or inks to achieve desired effects
- Trimming the art quilt with a rotary cutter for a raw-edged finish or sometimes adding a binding
- Gluing art quilts to fabric-covered art canvases for ease in hanging

YOUR ROAD MAP

Starter Guide to Creating Art Quilts gives you the chance of attempting a new form of art with a bit of a road map. You might want to look over the entire book (or road map) before you get started, but I encourage you to just get started. Select a project. Try one step at a time. You may not always feel like you know exactly where you are going. Trust that the next step will appear or make itself known as you take the journey. Trust the process. Trust that the fabric will talk to you and guide you in the process. Becoming better requires accepting the discomfort of not always knowing what you are doing but being willing to try new things anyway.

My desire with this book is to teach you the principles for creating collage quilts and to start you on your path as you make one or more of my projects. Art quilting is a journey, not a destination. In trying projects, you will pick up some tricks and tips that will supplement your current quilting skills and give you the confidence and knowledge needed if you choose to initiate some journeys with your own art quilts.

Design Inspiration

What can spark an idea for an art quilt?

- a scene in nature
- a photo in your own gallery
- a picture on an Internet site
- a greeting card
- a piece of artwork
- a beautiful piece of fabric
- a story or a poem
- a social issue
- something close to the heart

Inspiration for an art quilt can begin with appreciating the beauty of a flower in the landscaping outside a business or a restaurant (snap a picture!) or in seeing a picture of a red barn your friend posted on Facebook (ask to use it!). You may want to recapture the magic of a pet's smile or a special place you have visited. A seed can start with a painting on the wall at the doctor's office. Germination begins. Perhaps a piece of fabric in a quilt shop catches your eye. An idea for an art quilt is born. Visual representations like these spark seeds for art quilts. Life can be breathed into an art quilt that's inspired by a story or a social issue. Something that touches your heart points you toward wanting to turn that feeling into an art quilt. If you are deeply moved by a subject or a topic, that is a great inspiration for an art quilt. Here are some examples from my own life and art quilting experience:

Inspiration: Flowerbox outside Blueberry Haven in Grand Haven, Michigan

Result: *Blueberries and Bliss* art quilt

Inspiration: A picture posted on Facebook
(Photo by Sandy Kay Young, used with permission)

Inspiration: A beautiful piece of fabric

Result: *Fall* **art quilt**

Result: *Touch of Teal Pine Tree* **art quilt**

Following are some simple guiding steps I can share that will allow you to visualize these things that stir you and grow them into art quilts.

SAVE PICTURES AND INSPIRATIONS OF YOUR FAVORITE SUBJECTS

- Take pictures of things that inspire you. In your electronic and/or physical photo gallery, create a folder labeled "Future Art Quilt Ideas."
- Collect pictures from books, magazines, or Facebook and save them in a folder, album, or in an electronic file.
- Create a spot in your work area for collecting seed ideas (pictures and pleasing fabrics) that might bloom into future projects.

Using reference/study pictures to inform *Over the Cattails* **art quilt**

CONDUCT A STUDY OF PICTURES ON YOUR SUBJECT

When I want to create a new art quilt, I have learned that using reference pictures or conducting a study on my subject is essential. In the world of art, a "study" is looking at your subject in real life or looking at drawings, sketches, pictures, or paintings of your subject. A study can then include drawing, sketching, and taking notes in preparation for creating your piece of art.

HOW TO SEARCH FOR MORE PICTURES

I may have one picture of my subject, but more is better. To find additional reference pictures or to conduct a study on your topic, it's helpful to do an Internet search. Try these steps for image searches:

- Open a search engine
- Type in a search term like "cattails"
- Click on "Image" to look at all pictures
- Try including the word "painting" in your search (for example, "cattail painting")

SURROUND YOURSELF WITH PICTURES OF YOUR SUBJECT

Print the reference pictures that inspire you. When you are working on an art quilt, tape/clip your reference/study pictures to the wall. Surround your work area with these reference/study pictures.

THINK LIKE AN ARTIST

To draw the human body, artists are taught to study human anatomy. It stands to reason that if I want to capture the essence of a pumpkin in my fabric art, I should study pictures of pumpkins. If I am looking at a lot of pumpkin pictures, I'm getting general ideas about the way a pumpkin appears. We want to keep copyright laws in mind while using references; we should not directly copy or imitate an artist's work and should only use the images we see for general ideas. Get permission from artists, use public domain sources, and never use photos or pictures without changing them in significant ways so that it is not copying. If I have done a study on the subject and have several pictures for reference during the design phase, my results are more pleasing and pumpkin-like as well as unique to me.

Using a reference image of a pumpkin illustration

Creating an original sketch of the pumpkin

The final result: *October Twist* art quilt

Tools and Materials

In order to turn the ideas from the Design Inspiration chapter into art quilts, you'll want to look over these tools and materials for making it happen.

Domestic Sewing Machine
Generally set to 2.5 stitch width—I currently use a Viking Husqvarna 1 at home and a lighter Baby Lock Rachel for teaching travels. Look for these features and complementary tools:

- open-toe foot
- free motion foot (optional)
- sewing machine needles:
  - machine embroidery needles; 70/80
  - topstitch needles, optional
- quilting gloves with rubber fingers (aids gripping for stitching maneuverability)

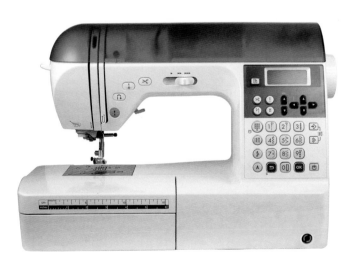

Two examples of domestic sewing machines. A lighter sewing machine is good to have if you want to take your projects on the road with you.

Threads

Look for:

- pretty colors
- thread shades that don't overpower fabric choices
- polyester invisible thread-smoke at times for less visibility
- bobbin threads:
  - ○ light gray or white
  - ○ dark tan like Aurifil 2370
  - ○ black
  - ○ matching color to top thread (occasionally needed)

Fabrics

You'll need:

- cotton backing fabric
- quilt batting, thin (with quilt basting spray) or Pellon® 971F or 987F fusible fleece
- quilting fabrics (see pp. 16–18)

Iron and Ironing Supplies

Start with what you have. Later consider the addition of a small iron (Steamfast SF717 Steam Iron). Also get your hands on the following tools:

- small ironing board and/or flannel-covered board—approx. 20" x 20" (50.8 x 50.8cm):
  - ○ a small ironing board is good for traveling and to keep next to your sewing machine for quick ironing right as you add pieces to sew down
  - ○ flannel-covered, foam-core, pin-able pressing board; good for parchment collaging
- Mary Ellen's Best Press spray sizing
- parchment paper, scrap paper from back of Wonder Under adhesive, or Teflon sheet:
  - ○ these sheets protect surfaces while ironing
  - ○ these sheets are perfect for use with "parchment paper collaging"
  - ○ parchment baking paper (not freezer paper!)
  - ○ scrap paper from the back of Wonder Under adhesive (I use this; it's free!)
- Teflon sheet (good, but smaller and more expensive)

Threads

Fabrics

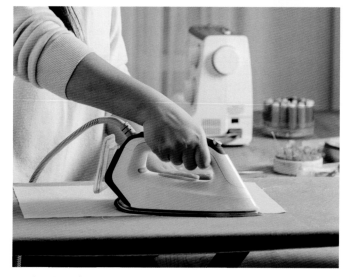

Ironing Supplies

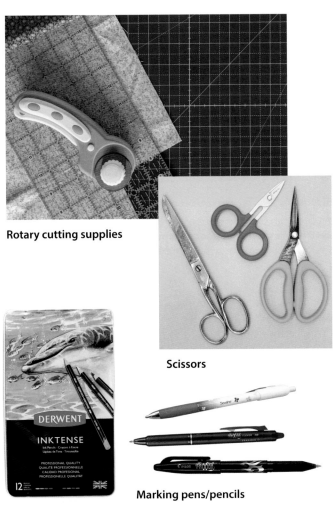

Rotary cutting supplies

Scissors

Marking pens/pencils

Adhesives

Pellon® 805 Wonder Under
Paper-Backed Fusible Web

Choose a size of blank cards,
such as A2 cards and envelopes

Rotary Cutting Supplies

You'll need:

- rotary cutters—30mm recommended; 45mm and 60mm are supplemental
- self-healing mat (Olfa is durable and easy on rotary cutters); sizes optional
- rotary cutting rulers; 2½" x 12½" (6.4 x 31.8cm) is a good starter, or 12½" x 12½" (31.8 x 31.8cm)

Scissors and Such

You'll need:

- Karen Kay Buckley 3¾" (approx. 9.5cm) curved scissors
- Karen Kay Buckley 6" (approx. 15.2cm) scissors
- paper scissors
- tweezers

Marking Pens/Pencils

You'll need:

- Pilot Ball Frixion iron-away pen
- Sewline White Ceramic Chalk Pencil
- Derwent Inktense Colored Pencils, starter set of 12

Adhesives

You'll need:

- Pellon® 805 Wonder Under—paper-backed fusible web
- large glue stick, e.g., Craft Bond, extra strength
- tacky glue
- Roxanne Glue Baste It
- quilt basting spray (if you use quilt batting)
- freezer paper

Blank Cards for Fiber Art Cards project

- A2 Cards—4¼" x 5½" (42 x 59.4cm) cardstock with envelopes

Stretched Art Canvas(es) for Four Seasons Art Quilts project

- 8" x 10" x ½" depth (20.3 x 25.4 x 1.5cm) depth

Landscape Art Quilt Basics

After looking over the suggested tools and materials from the previous chapter, it's time to think about turning the design inspiration ideas from the Design Inspiration chapter into art quilts. Once you decide on a design for an art quilt, there are some further actions to take and decisions to make.

A photo can take the place of a drawing as preparation for a sketch; this photo of a spot near our family cabin on Bois Blanc Island, Michigan, is a great example.

Step 1
Make a Drawing

In your sketch or drawing, include the composition, or components, of the major elements. For example, how wide is the sky or upper background area as compared to the lower area, and is the focal point more to the right or to the left? You can start with a very simple drawing, like the sketch for one of my earliest winter scenes. Later you may decide to take the time to sketch another drawing that includes a few more specific details in order to calculate fabric dimensions.

Sometimes, instead of drawing a picture, a photo can take the place of a drawing if it happens to include the composition and all of the design elements needed for the art quilt.

Winter Morning initial sketch

The final result!

Step 2
Choose the Medium (Cardstock or Fabric), Size, and Orientation

Medium (cardstock or fabric)—Usually, art quilts are made of fabric. Because I included a project using cardstock in this book, I will discuss information about that medium later as well.

Size—Whether you are making a fiber art scene on the front of a blank card or on an art quilt, you need to choose the size of cardstock you want or the size of art quilt you desire. For blank cards, I suggest A2 cards—4¼" x 5½" (42 x 59.4cm) cardstock with envelopes—as a good place to start.

As far as fabric art quilt decisions, do you want to go **small** or **big**?

The smallest fabric art I ever made was probably created to fit on a 2" x 3" (5.1 x 7.6cm) art canvas. I

Choose a size of art quilt—do you want to go super tiny, medium, or substantial?

Sometimes you will need to adapt a design to remove an element in order to make it smaller.

STANDARD CANVAS SIZES

INCHES	CENTIMETERS (approx.)
4" x 4"	10.2 x 10.2
5" x 3"	12.5 x 7.5
5" x 5"	12.5 x 12.5
6" x 4"	15 x 10.2
7" x 5"	17.5 x 12.5
8" x 8"	20 x 20
10" x 8"	25 x 20
10" x 10"	25 x 25
12" x 9"	30 x 23
12" x 12"	30 x 30
14" x 11"	35 x 30
16" x 12"	40 x 30
18" x 18"	45 x 45
18" x 24"	45 x 60
20" x 16"	50 x 40
20" x 20"	50 x 50
24" x 12"	60 x 30
24" x 36"	60 x 90
48" x 36"	120 x 90

commonly make bookmarks 2¼" x 7½" (5.7 x 19.1cm), and I make many other art quilts that fit on art canvases from 3" x 5" to 36" x 48" (7.5 x 12.5cm to 90 x 120cm). The most commonly available art canvas sizes are listed in the Standard Canvas Sizes chart.

I also recently made six 40" x 60" (approx. 1 x 1.5 meter) art quilts (without standard canvas art frames) to illustrate a story and a queen-sized art quilt of a beach scene for my bed. I'll let you in on a secret, though: small art quilts are easier to make. A nice beginning size art quilt that is easy to handle but with pieces that are not too small might be 8" x 10" (20.3 x 25.4cm) or even a 16" x 20" (40.6 x 50.8cm).

Orientation—Should the orientation of the quilt be square or rectangular? If it's rectangular, should you go with a landscape or portrait orientation? It's a matter of what best fits your inspiration and the elements of the design.

Choose a landscape or portrait orientation—your subject matter will often guide you to decide which one is appropriate.

Step 3
Start Making the Quilt Sandwich

A quilt sandwich is made up of cotton quilt backing, fuzzy batting, and the quilt top. As a starting point for creating your quilt sandwich, adhere the backing and batting together. There are two workable types of batting to use. The easiest to use is Pellon® 971F or 987F fusible fleece, which is ironed to the cotton backing. The second is a cotton batting (not puffy polyester) that you adhere to your cotton backing with quilt basting spray. Cut materials approximately ¼" (0.5cm) larger than your desired finished size to allow for shrinkage while ironing. Retrim after ironing.

If I am going to be making the starts of several quilt sandwiches, I usually adhere large-sized pieces of cotton backing and batting and cut this into smaller quilt sandwich sets.

If you are going to mount your art quilt on a fabric-covered canvas art frame, in most cases your quilt sandwich will need to be about 1"–3" (2.5 to 7.6cm)

Start the quilt sandwich with a backing and batting.

smaller in width and height than the canvas; for example, a 14" x 18" (35.6 x 45.7cm) quilt sandwich for a 16" x 20" (40.6 x 50.8cm) finished product. You will want to plan for this smaller sized quilt sandwich to achieve that 1"–3" (2.5 to 7.6cm) border surrounding and accentuating your art quilt.

Step 4
Audition and Choose Fabrics

I cannot stress enough the importance of choosing fabrics when making an art quilt. I have dedicated the next few pages to fabric selection. As you choose fabrics for an art quilt, here are some starting considerations for the fabrics you will use:

- types of fabric—mostly cottons, tightly woven, that will offer a minimum of edge-fraying
- fabric texture—all the same smooth texture or some other textures for added interest
- fabric color—match colors with cool or warm hues and maybe add some tints (lighter) and shades (darker)
- fabric pattern—use a real variety of patterns printed on the fabric that will complement the subject matter of the art quilt

Shopping for lots of pretty fabrics is essential for making beautiful art quilts—somebody has to do it!

Types of Fabric—Cottons are my fabrics of choice for art quilts. Cottons are easier to work with and less slippery than some other fabrics. Within the cotton category, flannels tend to have a large weave that will fray the most, quilting cottons a plain weave and a lot of body, and batiks a tight weave that will fray the least in the process of raw-edge collage quilting—almost like working

Here are some examples of quilting cottons, from the tightest weaves (smallest pieces, no fraying) to the largest weaves (bigger pieces, lots of fraying).

with paper. If I could find every fabric in a batik, I would use batiks almost exclusively. However, when I see the perfect color (hue), value (lightness or darkness), or a desirable design, print, or pattern in a piece of fabric, even if it isn't a batik, I must invite it to be a part of the art quilt. If you take the time to spray your fabrics with spray sizing before using them, they will fray less.

Fabric Texture—Most often, my cotton fabrics have a smooth texture. At times, an art quilt calls me to use something with a different texture, like gold lamé fabric for a sun, a linen for texture in a beach, sparkly tulle for some shine on the water, wool for a fluffy sheep, a bit of interesting trim, or other embellishments to create desired effects. Yes, these special fabrics and woven cottons, like linens and flannels, fray more than traditional quilting cottons. The edges of shiny fabrics and trims pose an array of problems. Keep this in mind if you don't want to battle fraying edges.

Fabric Color—I am mostly self-taught in the area of color theory. Here are some simple thoughts as you select fabric colors or hues. Cool colors include blue, green, and light purple. They tend to be calm and soothing. They remind us of water, sky, and even ice and snow. Warm colors are oranges, reds, and yellows; they can represent excitement and emotion. Think of sunlight and heat.

If blue (cool) was added to red as it was dyed, the red will read as just a little cooler. If yellow (warm) was added to red in the dying process, the red will read as just a little warmer. In auditioning reds for my project, I make my selections based on matching reds that read

Use different textures, like these linens and cork, for added interest.

Flannel and wool offer great tactile and visual texture.

Within a single color, there can be many shades and tones, lighter or darker.

From cool greens and blues to warm reds, think about how each color makes you feel.

the same—for example, reds that all read cooler because they read with a blueish hue, rather than reds that read with a yellowish hue. Does the gray have a yellow hue (warm) or a blue/silver hue (cool)? Is the green a yellow-green shade (warm) or a blue-green shade (cool)? Fabrics are "tinted" with white to make lighter tints and "shaded" with blacks to make darker shades. Remember that it's also possible to check the back of a fabric to see whether its back is just a lighter tint of the same hue—maybe you would prefer to use that side of the fabric in your project instead.

One more interesting thought about choosing fabric colors: medium "pretty colors" will also need "not as pretty" lights and/or darks to help the pretty colors shine.

Fabric Pattern—As far as what is printed or dyed on the *manufactured* (versus hand-dyed) cotton fabrics I use, there are loosely two broad categories: traditional quilting prints and landscape prints. I use many manufactured traditional quilting prints and some manufactured prints specifically designed for landscape art quilting. In examining traditional prints on quilting fabrics for use in art quilting, I try to choose a variety of printed patterns like dotted batiks, cross-hatches, minute florals, etc. You may want to explore using some beautiful hand-dyed fabrics. Painting or adding color to fabrics already purchased is another technique to consider. As a rule, do not use plain fabrics. Plain colors or solids appear flat, whereas patterned fabrics appear to have movement and warmth. A solid fabric also tends to stand out excessively when placed next to a patterned fabric.

Finding Fabrics—My warning to fellow art quilters: this practice of art quilting is very addictive and may result in strong urges to purchase seductive fabrics. It is extremely necessary to feed this addiction. You might ask, "How much fabric do you need or should you have?" MORE. How much should you buy of any one fabric? You might want to start out with an eighth or quarter yard or a fat quarter. However, if you think the fabric might make a good background for a scene, a half yard could be a good idea. Retracing your steps to repurchase more of a piece of fabric is a science, requiring artful moves and dedication. Where will you find the right fabric? Answer: your stash, your friends' stashes, local and not local quilt shops, trade shows, and online.

The backs of fabrics can provide a lighter tint of the same colors/hues, as you can see in the back and front sides of this bark pattern fabric.

Printed patterns on fabric—landscape art quilting designs versus traditional quilting designs. The fabrics on the left were designed specifically for art quilting. The fabrics on the right are traditional quilting fabrics that lend themselves to art quilting. You may already have some of these traditional quilting fabrics in your stash!

Support your local quilt shops!

Step 5

Back Fabric with Wonder Under

There are several different types of adhesives that can be used on the backs of fabrics to keep them in place as you stitch them down onto an art quilt. I prefer the highly versatile Pellon® 805 Wonder Under paper-backed fusible web. A fusible web is a manufactured fiber that will melt in mere seconds when heated. One side of the Wonder Under is paper-backed and ironable onto the back of a porous surface like fabric. Once the backed fabric is allowed to cool, the paper backing is removed, and the fabric is then ready to apply to your art quilt. Fabrics remain soft and easily sewable. Unlike using other fusible webs, no gooey substance sticks to your sewing machine needle. Wonder Under is machine washable and dryer and dry cleaner safe. At the time of writing, you can purchase a small package with two 15" (38cm)-wide yards for $7–$9 or 17" (43cm)-wide yardage for $3–$4 a yard; it is also available in options of 10-, 20-, or 35-yard package purchases.

You can easily back fabric measuring just a few inches or centimeters, a whole group of fabric strips cut the width of your project, or you can back fabric by the fat quarter or entire yardage.

If you want to back just enough fabric for one project, decide on the width of the project. Let's say you chose a 9" x 7" (22.9 x 17.8cm) art quilt. All fabric strips for the art quilt can be cut 9" (22.9cm) wide. Looking at your drawing, you decide on an approximate height of each 9"–wide (22.9cm) strip, plus even up to 1" (2.5cm) so that the strip isn't too narrow; e.g., a 9"–wide x 3"–high (22.9 x 7.6cm) strip could be cut 9" x 3½"–4" (22.9 x 8.9–10.2cm).

Quick Tip: Taking the time to spray fabrics with spray sizing or starch before applying Wonder Under will stiffen fabric and reduce fraying. I recommend using Mary Ellen's Best Press spray sizing.

Back fabrics with a product like Pellon® 805 Wonder Under Paper-Backed Fusible Web.

Backing a small amount of fabric with Wonder Under.

To save time, back all of your fabric pieces at once!

Look at your drawing to determine the amount of fabric to back.

Bring Your Project to Life

In the Landscape Art Quilt Basics chapter, I illustrated some of the basic preparations for art quilting. Your design inspiration is in your mind and you've made decisions as to the medium, size, and orientation of the project. Once you have a sketch/picture of the project, the backing and batting attached together, and adhesive adhered to your selected fabrics, the art quilt top can now start to come to life.

Step 1
Cut and Add Background

With a backing and batting quilt sandwich set atop your ironing surface (batting side up), you will next add the background of a scene's quilt top. The background of an art quilt can be very simple like the two-piece background I used as a backdrop for the vase of flowers, or the background might have several strips or pieces like the summer scene.

Add fabric strips from top to bottom. In this summer scene, I first pressed the sky strip across the top edge of the quilt batting.

Next, fussy cut the top edges of the remaining strips to give each strip a more natural, life-like appearance.

You will need to collage (arrange) together the background strips, from top to bottom, each overlapping the strip above until you have covered the batting from top to bottom. This is the time to evaluate whether your chosen fabrics really are playing nicely together. There is a sense of harmony when the layout or the composition of an art quilt "feels just right." I like to say that the fabrics will tell you when the colors or element placement in the art quilt feels right. It is like watching magic happen in front of your eyes. Make any needed adjustments and press.

A simple background can consist of one or two pieces.

A background can also consist of many layered strips, some cut simply, some cut with very specific edge shapes.

Here's an example of different unassembled and then assembled background options for a piece that is just 3" x 5" (7.6 x 12.7cm). You can pack a lot into the background!

Fussy cutting allows you to create more natural shapes using your backgrounds to imitate realistic landscapes.

Step 2
Stitch Down Background Layer

The manufactured pattern printed on each fabric tells me how to choose to stitch it down. Basically, stitch across each strip as closely to the top edge as you possibly can. Then, for several rows through the middle of each strip, you might stitch in rounded cloud-like meanders through a sky, loose waves over a hillside, tight waves on a sandy beach, spiked points for grass, etc. You should ensure that all the first-layer background strips are stitched down before you begin to add a second layer of elements such as trees or plants. You can see how difficult it would have been to stitch across the summer scene background strips with the trees in the way. Ask me how I know!

You can see the contrasting stitching on each layer here—smooth lines for the water, jagged spikes for the grass, etc.

Thread color and topstitch examples for this summer scene are

Light blue stitching in wavy cloud shapes across the blue sky

Medium tan across the top and in waves across the left hill

Olive green around the edges of the pines and up the middle of trees in pine-like spikes

Medium blue or shiny opalescent across the top and two to three more wavy rows through the blue waves

Medium tan or olive green in grass-like spikes up and down the right brown/tan/green grass clump

Light tan in dune-like waves across the top and through the sand-colored strip

Grass green in grass-like spikes across grassy strip in bottom right corner

Imagine trying to stitch the background consistently when the top layers (the trees) are already in place. It just won't work.

Step 3
Fussy Cut Other Design Elements

A second layer of art quilt elements gets pressed atop the stitched-down background layer. This summer scene's second layer is the tree trunk layer (not including the tree leaves). I rotary cut thin tree slivers from birch, black, or even brown fabric and arrange and press the trees onto the right side of the background.

You might want to take the time here to fussy cut elements that will be applied to the third layer, but set these third layer elements aside until later—don't stitch them down yet.

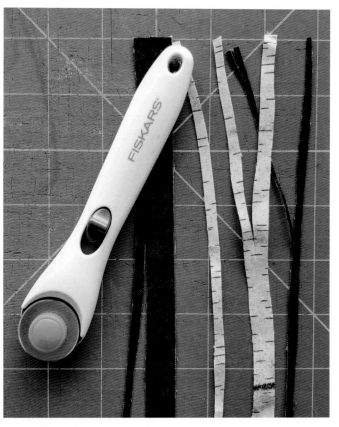

Fussy cut tiny leaves using tiny scissors and thin scrap strips (if possible).

Here are the tree trunks, ready to be artfully arranged onto the background.

Here are some examples of other fussy cut plants and trees that can be fun to add to nature scenes.

Step 4
Stitch Down Each Added Layer

Stitch down the elements of the second layer; in this case it's the layer of tree trunks. I stitched up one side of each tree trunk and down the other, "thread painting" secondary tree branches here and there. I stitched a wavering bark line up the centers of the wider trees. Drawing secondary branches with an iron-away pen is helpful when teaching yourself how to add more branches.

I pressed on the third layer (tree leaves only in this scene) after stitching down the tree trunks because I wanted to stitch down each added layer before adding more layers. I often add a third layer of low plants and stitch them in place. Small elements such as leaves need to be pressed firmly in place, but don't necessarily need to be stitched down.

The next layers to be stitched on are the tree trunks, followed by a third layer of leaves.

In this view of the back of the quilt, you can more clearly see the stitching choices made for each piece and layer.

Here's another example of final layer stitching, this one from *Reaching Upward, Panel #2*; 28" x 36" (72 x 96cm).

Step 5
Finish Your Quilt

Method One: Raw Edges—Press the art quilt top with moisture. Square up the sides of the art quilt with a ruler and rotary cutter. If desired, glue the art quilt to a fabric-covered art canvas with tacky glue. See "Covering a Stretched Art Canvas" on page 25.

Method Two: Adding a Binding—Press the art quilt top with moisture. Cut a ⅞" (2.2cm)–wide binding strip the length of the distance (circumference) around the edge of the art quilt, for example, 9" x 7" = 32+" (22.9 x 17.8cm = 91+cm). This fabric binding strip should be backed with Wonder Under—it's genius! Sew the binding to the front of the art quilt with a ¼" (.5cm) seam. Press flat on the front, then roll around and press to the back. If desired, glue the art quilt to a fabric-covered art canvas with tacky glue. **Note:** I taught myself the steps to bind quilts from a tutorial in a quilting book, and Internet tutorials are now very easy to follow, as well.

I've included two pictures of art quilts I named *Over the Cattails*—one with raw edges and one with edges bound.

Here is *Over the Cattails,* 16" x 20" (41.9 x 53.3cm), with a bound edge.

For comparison, here is *Over the Cattails,* 8" x 10" (20.3 x 25.4cm), with raw-edged finishing.

Raw edges, as done here for *Summer Breezes*, is a viable option that requires minimal work.

Step 6
Covering a Stretched Art Canvas
(optional for mounting an art quilt)

In order to finish a project this way, you'll need a stretched art canvas, a large glue stick (a small glue stick takes too long) not of the "repositionable" variety, and fabric to cover the canvas. Choose a color of fabric that will complement and border the colors in your art quilt. For ½" (1.5cm)–deep stretched art canvas frames, cut fabric 2½" (3.8cm) larger than the dimension of the canvas frame; for example, for an 8" x 10" (20.3 x 25.4cm) frame, cut the fabric 10½" x 12½" (26.7 x 31.8cm).

1. Using a large glue stick, with the fabric face down, apply glue liberally in a 1"–2" (2.5–5.1cm) swath around all four outside edges on the back of the fabric. Place the art canvas face down in the center of the fabric with the wet glue applied. Work quickly, as the glue is fast-drying.

2. Fold the longest edges over two parallel sides of the frame, pulling taut.

3. On one of the short ends, fold in the end fabric, then make a perpendicular line across the edge of the frame. This will leave you with four diagonal tabs that need glue applied to the inside surfaces. After applying glue to the four tabs, fold these tabs over the short edge of the frame.

4. Repeat step 3 on the opposite short end.

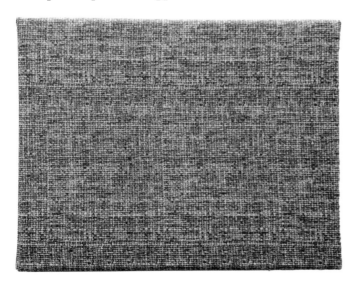

Here's the completed fabric canvas!

Projects

Fiber Art Cards

Once you try making one of these cards, you may not be able to stop making them. They really are quite easy and so much fun to create. You can get a lot of ideas for designs by just looking at the pictures of these card samples. I've shared a few categories for cards, but really, the sky's the limit.

Basic Supplies

- NO sewing machine needed
- A2 cards—4¼" x 5½" (42 x 59.4cm) cardstock with envelopes
- Small, sharp scissors
- Tweezers
- Rotary cutter, ruler, and mat
- Iron and board
- Parchment paper or Teflon ironing sheet
- Small iron and ironing board
- Fabrics of your choice
- Pellon® 805 Wonder Under fusible web
- Mary Ellen's Best Press spray sizing

Topic Idea: Landscapes

Topic Idea: Flowers

Topic Idea: Leaves

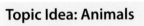

Topic Idea: Animals

Topic Idea: Christmas

Background Option #1—a plain card; no background piece behind fussy cut pieces/elements

Background Option #2—with fabric rectangle background behind fussy cut pieces/elements

Background Option #3—with a multi-strip background behind fussy cut pieces/elements

Option #1
Plain Card with No Background Piece

1. Fussy cut desired elements for your card from colored fabrics stiffened with Mary Ellen's Best Press spray sizing and backed with Pellon® 805 Wonder Under (see page 19).

2. With the cardstock right side up on the ironing surface, collage/arrange the elements atop the cardstock, gently cover with a piece of parchment paper, and press.

Option #2
Fabric Rectangle Background

1. Stiffen your colored fabrics with Mary Ellen's Best Press spray sizing and adhere Pellon® 805 Wonder Under (see page 19) to the back of the fabric for the background rectangle and the desired elements of the scene.

2. Cut the fabric for the background to a 3¼" x 4½" (8.3 x 11.4cm) rectangle and fussy cut the desired elements for your card.

3. With the cardstock right side up on the ironing surface, center the fabric rectangle atop the cardstock, gently cover with a piece of parchment paper, and press.

4. Collage/arrange the fussy cut fabric elements atop the background rectangle, gently cover with a piece of parchment paper, and press.

Here I've cut many evergreens to place on top of simple rectangular backgrounds.

Always remember to protect the surface of the cardstock when pressing.

Fussy cutting Christmas elements

Fussy cutting floral elements

Option #3
Multi-Strip Background Card

To make this kind of card, you will use a piece of parchment paper and a hot iron to collage/arrange the four background strips onto the parchment, let it cool, and peel off the background you are creating.

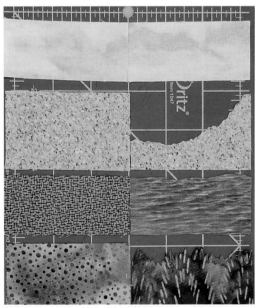

1. Stiffen your colored fabrics with Mary Ellen's Best Press spray sizing and adhere Pellon® 805 Wonder Under (see page 19) to the fabrics. Sub-cut the fabrics (you can see several options shown here) into the following sizes. Sky: 3¼" x 1½" (8.3 x 3.8cm); water: 3¼" x 1¾" (8.3 x 4.4cm); sand: 3¼" x 2¼" (8.3 x 5.7cm) diagonal; ground cover: 3¼" x 1¾" (8.3cm x 4.4cm). If desired, fussy cut the details now as well (see step 5). Then fussy cut a rolling edge off the top of the water and off the left bottom corner of the water. Fussy cut pebbles off the top of the tan sand bowl, and spikes off the top of the ground cover. Leave the sky strip untrimmed.

2. Atop Teflon/parchment paper, slightly overlap the four background strips, starting with the sky, then the water, then the sand, and lastly the bottom ground cover. Press. Allow to cool. Rip the combined background strip set off the parchment paper like a Band-aid.

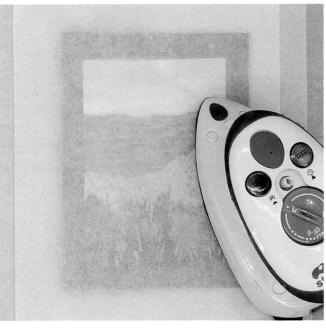

3. Square up the approximately 3¼" x 4½" (8.3 x 11.4cm) fabric strips with a rotary cutter and ruler.

4. With the cardstock right side up on the ironing surface, center the fabric background scene atop the cardstock, cover with a piece of parchment paper, and press.

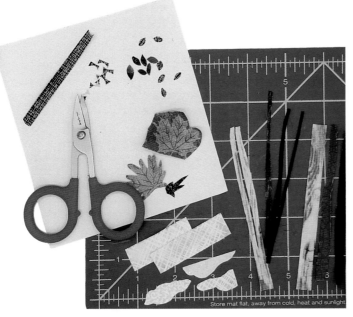

5. If you haven't already, fussy cut two plants, two white pieces for clouds, three colors for 4½" (11.4cm) trees, and green for the tree leaves.

6. Collage/arrange the plants, clouds, and trees in place atop the multi-layered background scene (You can see how different colors and patterns can be used to create different effects.) Gently cover with a piece of parchment paper. Press. Now add leaves to the trees. Tweezers are good friends here. Gently cover with parchment paper. Press.

Cactus Bookmarks

Bookmarks—where the love of art quilting and the passion for reading converge! My first career was as a teacher and literacy specialist at the K–12 and college levels. My second career is as an art quilter. The idea for my first bookmark probably surfaced when I needed a project for elementary children to experience art quilting. A small project works well for groups like this. Scraps left over from other art quilting projects lend themselves to bookmark-sized creations, so I make a lot of bookmarks. I often come up with different designs for bookmarks and I sell tons of bookmarks in galleries and shows. Bookmarks also work well as thank-you gifts or in sympathy cards, and for the curious, I carry several bookmarks in my purse to show as examples of art quilting.

Each spring I journey to the Southwest where we have family. The Sonoran Botanical Gardens in Phoenix and other desert areas are an inspiration in the springtime. I created this cactus bookmark to have a regional design to offer an area quilting club. It is an easy-to-accomplish and inexpensive project to teach the art of landscape quilting and the step-by-step photos show how versatile these designs can be when you use different colors and fabrics for the elements.

Measurement: 2¼" x 7½" (5.7 x 19.1cm)

Basic Supplies
- Sewing machine (open-toe foot recommended)
- Small, sharp scissors
- Tweezers
- Rotary cutter, ruler, and mat
- Iron and board
- Teflon sheet/parchment paper
- Iron-away/erasable marking pen; for example, Pilot Ball Frixion
- Fabrics and thread of your choice (see Fabric and Thread, on the right)
- Cotton backing: 2½" x 8" (6.4 x 20.3cm)
- Batting: 2½" x 8" (6.4 x 20.3cm)
  - Option 1—Pellon® 971F or 987F fusible fleece
  - Option 2—Thin cotton batting
- Quilt basting spray if using thin cotton batting rather than fusible fleece
- Pellon® 805 Wonder Under fusible web: approx. 5" x 10" (12.7 x 25.4cm) rectangle
- Thin cardboard or freezer paper: approx. 2" x 5" (5.1 x 12.7cm) rectangle
- Mary Ellen's Best Press spray sizing (optional)
- Sewing gloves (optional)

Fabric and Thread
Fabric
- Sky (pale blue): 2¼" x 2¼" (5.7 x 5.7cm)
- Red Mountain (rusty brown): 2¼" x 2¼" (5.7 x 5.7cm)
- Green Bushes: 1" x 2¼" (2.5 x 5.7cm)
- Spotted Sand: 2" x 2¼" (5.1 x 5.7cm)
- Lighter Sand: 2" x 2¼" (5.1 x 5.7cm)
- Brown Ground: 1" x 2¼" (2.5 x 5.7cm)
- Cactus (green): 1½" x 4½" (3.8 x 10.2cm)
- Yucca plant (dark sage green): each 1¼" x 1" (3.2 x 2.5cm)
- Yucca plant (light sage green): each 1¼" x 1" (3.2 x 2.5cm)
- Twigs (brown): 1½" x 1½" (3.8 x 3.8cm)
- Rocks (browns/tans): less than 1" (2.5cm)

Thread
- Pale blue; for example, Sulky 1223
- Dark tan; for example, Aurifil 2370
- Sage or olive green
- Light tan
- Medium honey brown
- Medium green
- Black and white bobbin thread

1. Start making your quilt sandwich. Iron or spray together a 2½" x 8" (6.4 x 20.3cm) cotton backing to a 2½" x 8" (6.4 x 20.3cm) batting, either by ironing together if using Pellon® 971F or 987F fusible fleece or by fusing with quilt basting spray if using a thin cotton batting. (See Start Making the Quilt Sandwich on page 16 for additional tips.) With rotary cutter and ruler, trim the quilt sandwich to 2¼" x 7½" (5.7 x 19.1cm).

2. Using Pellon® 805 Wonder Under iron-on adhesive, back a small amount of each of the fabrics you have chosen for this bookmark project. Or, if you plan to make only one bookmark, using a 5" x 10" (12.7 x 25.4cm) rectangle of Wonder Under is more than adequate to back all the dimensions of the precut fabric squares and rectangles. See Steps for Backing Fabric with Wonder Under on page 19. **Optional:** As an aid in stiffening the colored fabrics and to reduce fraying, pre-iron all fabrics with Mary Ellen's Best Press spray sizing.

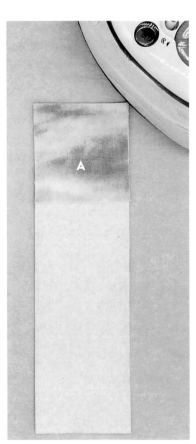

3. You will create the landscape picture on top of the 2¼" x 7½" (5.7 x 19.1cm) lining and batting set, with batting side up and lining side down. Press 2¼" (5.7cm) sky piece (A) across the top third of the batting.

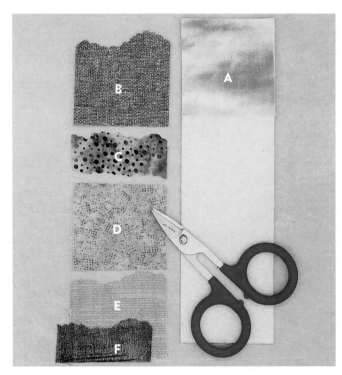

4. Fussy or rolling cut (making right sides higher than the left) across the tops only of the Red Mountain (B), the Light Sand (E), and the Brown Ground strips (F). Fussy or rolling cut across the top and bottom of the Green Bushes (C) strip. There's no need to fussy cut Spotted Sand (D).

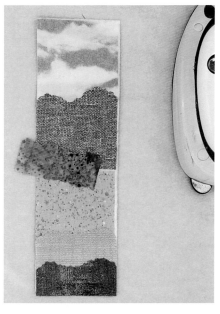

5. Atop the bottom area of the batting, arrange/collage strips B through F, starting by overlapping the bottom of the sky so that they fill the space and down to the bottom edge of the batting. Add the green bushes strip last. Press.

6. Topstitch each background strip from top to bottom with matching thread colors to make the background for your scene. Stitch just inside the top edge of each strip and meander once or twice across the middles of the strips.

7A. **OPTION 1**: CACTUS TEMPLATE WITH FREEZER PAPER. Trace the cactus template onto a small rectangle of freezer paper, waxy side down. With paper scissors, rough **trim** around this paper cactus design, leaving a ¼" (0.6cm) or so edge. Put parchment paper down first to protect the ironing board, then place the green Cactus fabric Wonder Under side down and center the freezer paper design (waxy side down) on top of the green fabric. Press. Allow the green freezer paper set to cool. Rip the freezer paper and fabric **set** off the parchment paper like a Band-Aid. Cut out this cactus design and remove the freezer paper.

7B. **OPTION 2**: CACTUS TEMPLATE WITH DIRECT TRACING. Trace the cactus template onto paper or parchment paper. Cut out the template. Trace around the cactus template onto the green Cactus fabric. Cut the cactus element from the green fabric.

Cactus template

LAYERS FOR TEMPLATE WITH FREEZER PAPER

5th layer —**IRON**

4th layer—**FREEZER PAPER**
(waxy side down)

3rd layer—**FABRIC**
(Wonder Under side down)

2nd layer—**PARCHMENT PAPER**

1st layer—**IRONING BOARD**

8. Fussy cut Yucca plants, Twig , and Rocks from fabrics. Use erasable pen to sketch some elements on the fabric pieces before cutting. It is not cheating to search the Internet for yucca plant images, etc., to better visualize how plants grow.

9. Collage/arrange these floral elements onto the bottom area of the background and press. I've shown just a few of the different fabric options here.

10. Topstitch around the edges of these elements with matching thread colors.

11. Press the entire scene with moisture. Square up the sides of the picture with a ruler and rotary cutter. Bind the edge with black thread using a blanket stitch or satin stitch setting on your sewing machine.

GENERIC BOOKMARK DIRECTIONS

1. Make/adhere a 2¼" x 7½" (5.7 x 19.1cm) cotton backing and batting quilt sandwich set.

2. Use fabrics backed with Pellon® 805 Wonder Under fusible web.

3. Cut any background strips 2¼" (5.7cm) wide.

4. Press top/sky piece to top edge of fuzzy batting of the quilt sandwich.

5. Generally fussy cut top background edges of additional strips.

6. Collage/arrange #2 strip overlapping the bottom of the sky, #3 strip overlapping bottom of #2 strip, etc., to fill space to the bottom of the batting. Press.

7. Stitch down these background strips with coordinating colored threads.

8. Fussy cut and add extra elements. Press in place.

9. Stitch down extra elements.

10. Damp press.

11. Square with rotary cutter and ruler.

12. Bind edge with black thread using a blanket stitch or satin stitch setting on your sewing machine.

Touch of Teal **bookmarks**

Birches in Blue and Green **bookmarks**

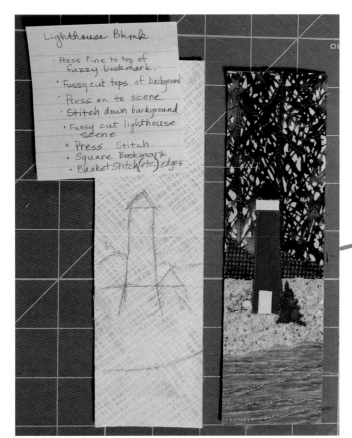

Lighthouse **bookmark (with sketch)**

Blues of Winter bookmark (with cutting samples)

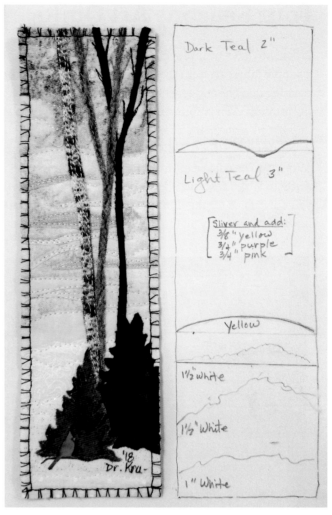

Dark Teal 2"

Light Teal 3"

[Sliver and add:
3/8" yellow
3/4" purple
3/4" pink]

Yellow

1½" White

1½" White

1" White

Winter Morning bookmark (with sketch)

Four Seasons Art Quilts

Prepare to have fun! You will amaze yourself at how easy it is to bring to life a collaged landscape scene as a simple fabric art quilt (beginner level). Soon after I began making collaged landscape art quilts, I started creating designs and teaching classes of the four changing seasons. Participants making this project in my art quilt classes found the project to be much easier than it looked. Their friends and family were most impressed with their efforts.

My original 10" x 8" (25.4 x 20.3cm) quilts of the four seasons were each unique, with varying levels of difficulty. The easiest of the four seasons designs, and the easiest project I've ever taught, turned out to be the *Autumn Warmth* scene. Nature gives us the beauty of the changing seasons. I decided that rather than give you one choice for the third project in this book, I would give you four variations of the same scene! Choose to make just one or try all four.

Outside Measurement: 10" x 8" (25.4 x 20.3cm)

Inside Measurement: 9" x 7" (22.9 x 17.8cm)

Thread

- Winter: light gray, bright white, dark green, medium green, black
- Spring: light blue, matching greens, medium tan, white, dark gray or #442 Madeira, black
- Summer: sky blue, olive green, grass green, medium tan, light tan, water blue or opalescent, dark gray or #442 Madeira, black
- Autumn: light tan, medium tan, sage green, dark green, golden, rust, dark brown, medium brown

Basic Supplies

- Sewing machine (open-toe foot recommended)
- Small, sharp scissors
- Tweezers
- Rotary cutter, ruler, and mat
- Iron and board
- Teflon sheet/parchment paper
- Iron-away/erasable marking pen; for example, Pilot Ball Frixion
- Large glue stick and tacky/fabric glue
- Pellon® 805 Wonder Under fusible web: 9" x 17" (22.9 x 43.3cm) strip
- Cotton backing (per season): 9" x 7" (22.9 x 17.8cm) (add ¼" [0.6cm] for shrinkage)
- Batting (per season): 9" x 7" (22.9 x 17.8cm) (add ¼" [0.6cm] for shrinkage)
  - Option 1—Pellon® 971F or 987F fusible fleece
  - Option 2—Thin cotton batting
- Quilt basting spray if using thin cotton batting rather than fusible fleece
- Thread of your choice (see Fabric, below, and Thread, on the left)
- Mary Ellen's Best Press spray sizing
- Sewing gloves (optional)
- Stretched art canvas: 8" x 10" (20.3 x 25.4cm)
- Art canvas fabric (per season): 12½" x 10½" (31.8 x 26.7cm); maroon for Winter, green for Spring, blue for Summer, brown for Autumn

FABRIC STRIPS	SIZE	WINTER	SPRING	SUMMER	AUTUMN
A. Sky	9" x 3" (22.9 x 7.6cm)	Dull teal, mottled	Pale blue	Bright blue	Tan
B. Trees/Hill Line	9" x 1½" (22.9 x 3.8cm)	Evergreen trees	Blooming trees	Evergreen trees	Sage green hillside
C. Left Bushes/Hill	5¼" x 3" (13.3 x 7.6cm)	Medium gray-green	Medium green	Medium brown dune	Dark army green
D. Right Grasses	5" x 2" (12.7 x 5.1cm)	Medium green or silver	Spring green	Dune grasses	Tan grasses
E. Top Ground	9" x 1½" (22.9 x 2.5cm)	White snow	Stones for wall	Mixed blue water	Golden grasses
F. Middle Ground	9" x 1½" (22.9 x 3.8cm)	White snow	Minty green	Sandy shoreline	Rust
G. Bottom Ground	8" x 1" (20.3 x 2.5cm)	Gray snow	Tan pebbles	Green grasses	Dark brown
H. Clouds	6" x 1½" (15.2 x 3.8cm)	None	White	White	None
I. Tree Trunks	1" x 7" (2.3 x 17.8cm)	Birch trees	Birch trees	Birch trees	Medium brown
J. Tree Trunks	½" x 7" (1.5 x 17.8cm)	Black	Black	Black	Dark brown
K. Plants	3" x 3" (7.6 x 7.6cm)	Twigs (or stitching)	Plants/tulip leaves	Variegated green leaves	Fall leaves
L. Extra	1" x 1" (2.5 x 2.5cm)	Red for berries	Tulip colors		

1. Start making your quilt sandwich. Iron or spray together a 9" x 7" (22.9 x 17.8cm) cotton backing and a 9" x 7" (22.9 x 17.8cm) batting, either by ironing together if using Pellon® 971F or 987F fusible fleece or fusing with quilt basting spray if using a thin cotton batting. Cut the backing and batting materials approximately ¼" (0.6cm) larger to allow for shrinkage while ironing. See Start Making the Quilt Sandwich on page 16.

2. Using Pellon® 805 Wonder Under fusible web, cut a 9" x 17" (22.9 x 43.3cm) strip and back all fabrics (except the large piece of fabric for frame covering), following the manufacturer's directions or see Steps for Backing Fabric with Wonder Under on page 19. Optional: As an aid in stiffening fabrics and to reduce fraying, pre-iron all colored fabrics with Mary Ellen's Best Press spray sizing.

3. Using a large glue stick, glue a 12½" x 10½" (31.8 x 26.7cm) fabric rectangle to the sides and back edges of the 10" x 8" (25.4 x 20.3cm) art canvas. See Covering a Stretched Art Canvas on page 25. You will create the landscape picture on top of the 9" x 7" (22.9 x 17.8cm) lining and batting set, with batting side up and lining side down.

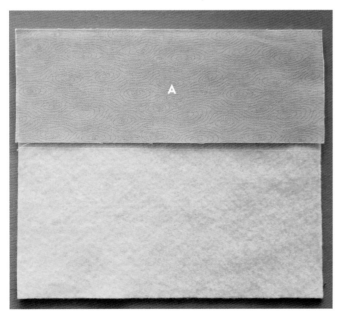

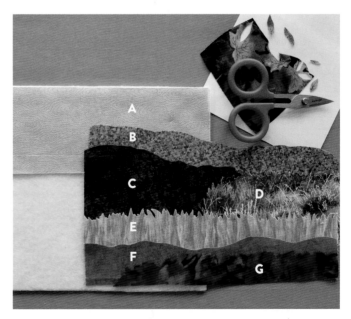

4. Press the 3" (7.6cm) sky piece (A) across the top third of the batting.

5. Fussy or rolling cut across the tops of strips B through G.

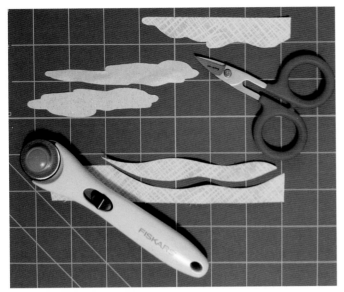

6. For spring or summer scenes, fussy or rotary cut cloud shapes from the white 6" x 1½" (15.2 x 3.8cm) strip.

7. Atop the bottom area of the batting, arrange or collage the six strips B through G, starting by overlapping the bottom of the sky and filling the space down to the bottom edge of the batting. Press the pieces in place. If using clouds, collage and press the clouds on top of the sky area.

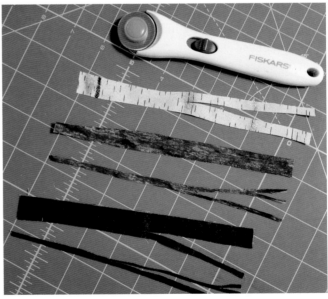

8. Topstitch each piece from top to bottom with matching thread colors to make the background for your scene. Stitch just inside the top edge of each strip, meander across the middles of the strips, and stitch in spike-like motions for elements such as grass and pines.

9. Rotary cut trees from the fabrics. Cut a very narrow strip lengthwise, flaring one end a bit wider than the other. With the narrowest end at the top and the widest part toward you, rotary cut upwards, slivering some branches out of the wider area of the strip.

10. Arrange and press the trees on the right side of the scene. Topstitch the trees in matching thread colors. Notice that a wavy line of stitching up the center of the trunk adds a bark-like quality. For added interest, you can use an iron-away pen to draw in some secondary branches for fussy stitching.

11. Add any twigs, plants, leaves, flowers, or berries. It's your choice—simply press them in place or choose to add stitching atop the elements.

12. Press the entire scene with moisture. Square up the sides of the picture with a ruler and rotary cutter. Glue (with tacky glue or a large glue stick) the back of the picture to the art canvas.

Four Seasons, Winter

Four Seasons, Winter **stitching closeups**

Four Seasons, Spring

Four Seasons, Spring **stitching closeups**

Four Seasons, Summer

Four Seasons, Summer stitching closeups

Four Seasons, Autumn **stitching closeups**

About the Author

Dr. Susan Jenae Kruszynski lives in Muskegon, Michigan, and is an award-winning art quilt designer, teacher, and gallery artist. At the age of 8, Susan's maternal grandmother handed her an embroidery project. That initiated her over 50-year experimentation with fabrics to produce colorful artistic creations. She began landscape fiber art design with collage art quilts in 2014. A native of Michigan, her works are often inspired by the trees and woodlands along the Lake Michigan shoreline.

Susan currently divides her time between creating original collaged art quilt designs, teaching art quilting classes in and around the state of Michigan, marketing her fiber art at shows and exhibitions, and running her Quilting Fabrics in Time business; she only just recently retired from a job as a literacy specialist at Muskegon Community College. Susan uses her 40+ years of K–College level teaching experience and her Ph.D. in Education to provide fun and easy learning experiences in classes and with online instruction. Her art quilts range in sizes from 3" x 5" (7.6 x 12.7cm) to 40" x 60" (101 x 152cm).

By hand cutting, collaging, pressing, and machine stitching pieces of fabric together, Susan creates art quilts that look like paintings. With this book, she hopes to add value to her readers' lives by teaching the principles for creating collage art quilts and helping them to make one or more projects from this book. Perhaps you will experience the joy of art quilting and feel emboldened and secure enough to create additional art quilts of your own.

For more inspiration from Susan's work, be sure to check out her second book, *Art Quilts Made Easy*, to be released in 2022. Also, feel free to view more of her artwork found in the gallery on her website.

AWARDS

- Grand Rapids ArtPrize Nine 2017 (TOP 25), *Reaching Upward*; Eleven 28" x 36" (71.1 x 91.4cm) story panels
- Michigan Education Association (MEA) Art Acquisitions Purchase Exhibition, *Kruszing Thru the Seasons;* 12" x 42" (30.5 x 106.7cm) in 2018 and *Teal Trees*; 24" x 36" (61 x 91.4cm) in 2019 (JURORS' CHOICE AWARD and PURCHASE AWARDS)
- Grand Haven Lighthouse Quilt Guild Show, 1st PLACE, *Teal Trees*; 24" x 36" (61 x 91.4cm) in 2018 and *Resilience #1*; 40" x 60" (101.6 x 152.4cm) in 2019
- Michigan Education Association (MEA) Art Acquisition and Purchase Exhibition Brochure cover design for 2020—*Teal Trees;* 24" x 36" (61 x 91.4cm)

GALLERIES

- Gallery Uptown—Grand Haven, Michigan
- Muskegon Museum of Art—Muskegon, Michigan
- Newaygo County Council for the Arts, Artsplace—Fremont, Michigan
- Studio 2 Gallery—Montague, Michigan

MEDIA

- Website—*www.quiltingfabricsintime.com*
- Facebook—Quilting Fabrics in Time—*https://www.facebook.com/Quilting-Fabrics-In-Time-1694599947516014*
- Instagram—*www.instagram.com/quiltingfabricsintime*
- Etsy—*https://www.etsy.com/shop/ArtQuiltsbySusan*

Resources

Loveless, Ann. *Landscape Quilt Arts, Step-by-Step: Learn Fast, Fusible Fabric Collage*. Concord, CA: C&T Publishing, 2015.

> Excellent book with an easy-to-follow 22-page tutorial on collage quilting. This book originally taught me the process of collage landscape art quilting. Big note: Ann uses Steam-a-Seam 2 for a substance to adhere the fabric to the batting, and I use Pellon® 805 Wonder Under fusible web to back all my fabric.

Eckmeier, Karen. *Accidental Landscapes: Surprisingly Simple Quilted Scenes*. Kent, CT: The Quilted Lizard, 2008.

> This book gave me artistic advice on creating landscape art quilts. Karen folds over each piece of fabric so that there are no raw edges (which I do not). She has an excellent section on four easy approaches to landscaping: using photos for inspiration and incorporating an actual photo into the landscape, using favorite colors and fabrics, winter effects like using tulle, and black and white monochrome scenes.

Zieman, Nancy and Sewell, Natalie. *The Art of Landscape Quilting*. Iola, WI: Krause Publications, 2007.

> I learned so much about cutting and adding either paint, markers, or chalk to enhance my landscape scenes. The book discusses using photos for inspiration, choosing fabrics, and the three techniques of messy cutting, fussy cutting, and gluing. Lots of examples of trees and flower scenes.

Becker, Joyce R. *Quick Little Landscape Quilts: 24 Easy Techniques to Create a Masterpiece*. Concord, CA: C&T Publishing, 2011.

> You'll learn lots of useful techniques for landscape quilting: how to start, machine embroidery techniques, using inks, embellishing landscapes, adding photos, and more.

Greir, Cathy. *Lovely Landscape Quilts: Using Strings and Scraps to Piece and Appliqué Quilts*. Ft. Collins, CO: Interweave Press, 2014.

> Cathy uses a strip technique to landscape quilting. Even if you do not choose to use that technique, you will learn a lot about layering different colors. She gives a great lesson on making a leaf collage (little pieces of fabric cut into confetti) to have a tree be multi-layered and more three-dimensional.

Stein, Susan. *The Complete Photo Guide to Art Quilting*. Gloucester, MA: Quarry Books, 2012.

> Want to get out of the box and into a bit more modern world—or at least explore new possibilities? By looking through the pages of designs in this book, you will breathe in ideas for mounting your art in unique ways. The book inspired me to practice the art of making simple leaves and tree trunks.

Durbin, Pat. *Fabric + Paint + Thread = Fabulous*. Bothell, WA: That Patchwork Place, 2009.

> One of my students recently introduced me to this book! The author shares stitching tidbits and techniques with which to experiment. Painting on your landscape art pieces with thread or with paint/markers can take your projects to a new level. For example, check out "thread motifs" that can make trees look more leafy/realistic and water or skies more lifelike.

Taylor, Emily. *Collage Quilter: Essentials for Success with Collage Quilts*. Sandy, UT: The Collage Quilter, 2019.

> Emily Taylor, former mural artist turned art quilter, provides some basics in color theory in the first third of this book that are easily understandable.